Between Twilight

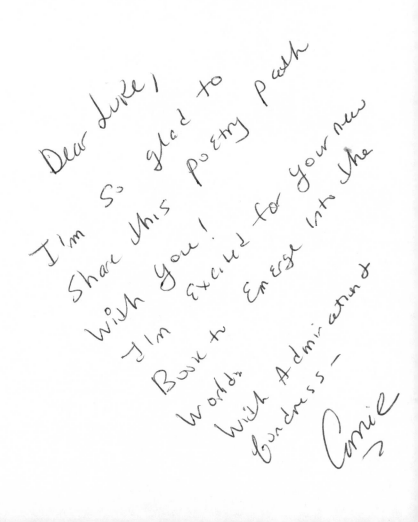

Dear Luke,

I'm so glad to
share this poetry path
with you! I'm
excited for your new
Book to emerge into the
world.

with Admiration &
fondness —

Carrie

Between Twilight

Connie Post

NYQ Books™

The New York Quarterly Foundation, Inc.
Beacon, New York

NYQ Books™ is an imprint of The New York Quarterly Foundation, Inc.

The New York Quarterly Foundation, Inc.
P. O. Box 470
Beacon, NY 12508

www.nyq.org

First Edition

Set in New Baskerville

Layout and Design by Raymond P. Hammond

Cover Image: Copyright © 2018 by istock/agsandrew

Author Photo: Casey Henshaw, Little Rae Photography

Library of Congress Control Number: 2023931133

ISBN: 978-1-63045-097-7

For Erika
You find me at every
creased corner
of my heart

Contents

Between Twilight

Floor Plan

I want to live in a house
where the rooms are half made
the walls
thin as moth wings

a place where
no one can be trapped
in a room
with one persecutor
the one with the dark hands
the open mouth

there will be no bugs
crushed into the corners
of the night

the plans should not include
hall lights
or closets

the floors
always spotless
clear as a glass bottom boat

the entry way
should be built
on salient sand

I will find a vase
that holds my conscious self
place it carefully
on the translucent table with no legs

I step into my room
find the architect
with his broken fingers
and hands

he tells me
"I am ready now"

What to Say

Why speak of sorrow
when it slips out
of the mouths
of the broken birds
clutching to the telephone lines

why speak of regret
when the black feral cat
runs into the hedges
upon your turn into the drive

why speak of rage
when the car skids
on the slick ice
in the opposite direction
of your intentions

why tell anyone
about the secret paralysis
that seizes you during sleep

why speak to the
rabid moon
when the crickets
are muted
and starving
on the dark

After the Sixth Day

The heat wave is nearing its end
we take the dogs
for a walk at dusk
it's the only time their paws
won't burn on the pavement

you stop at the corner
your knee is bothering you again
you say "I'll wait here"

I go to the end of the long street
without you

the dogs look back
over and over
but I pull them towards me

the moon falls on us
and I imagine
what it would be like
if you were gone

on the way back
I pass the same wilted flower beds

the dogs see you in the distance
prance towards you
as if you have been gone forever
"will it be like this"
I wonder
when I turn the long
unmarked curve of a fallen road
the light leaving
the road darkening
the gravity relentless as heat

you
quietly beckoning
while the trees learn to bend

Directions

I follow
the written directions
beside me
on the passenger seat

I find the house
by reading the names
of each street

off the main thoroughfare
I take two lefts
one slight right

it says, if I pass the stop sign
I've gone too far

weeks pass
and soon
I know how to get there
by instinct
weeks become years

I no longer look at the signs
instead, listen to my favorite radio station
and turn each corner
without a single thought

the way
I turn into you at night
the street lamps
blur to skin

the cul-de-sac of
your curved back

the curb of your hip bones
and my skin warming,
coasting into yours

Cooling Trend

I woke
and all the seasons
had been rearranged

fall was before summer
– large orange leaves could be found
clogging the opening to the vernal equinox

July started to crack
like frozen pipes
March found itself
praying to the global warming gods
begging for permission

spring came after summer
and the humidity
found its way into every month
until the earth sweltered
beneath the self-made
ozone blanket

I forced myself back to sleep
and when I woke again
I saw the same ravens
traveling in the same patterns
from decades ago

I sit quietly now
on the ledge of solstice
and wonder how to mark a tree
so I can be found

The Fire Is Ten Percent Contained

A crow flies
out of the smoke-filled sky

I've read
that they recognize faces
and for a moment
I wonder if this lonely bird sees mine

a crow cannot shelter in place
or find a face covering

they cannot wash their claws
in the polluted river near our house

they fly over us
not noticing the death toll

not able to pull us out
of our own ruined houses

I wash my hands
until they crack

I check air particulate readings
and listen for dry lightning
as evening descends

I wonder where the birds
sleep at night
while the grass burns
through the singed fields
or our sins

how far must they ascend
to forget our faces

Bound to Repeat It

There are atrocities in the body
millions of skin cells
sloughing off every moment

we start
by losing our amniotic lives
leaving the placenta behind
falling into and out of
this oxygenated existence

we exile ourselves
from the connective tissue
of our worn selves
we turn away from
the genocide of blocked arteries

our voices
fall out of us
into a thousand
shallow rooms

we brush our teeth at night
scraping away enamel
as if it will return

we turn down the bed
lose another strand of hair
never notice the mass graves
beneath our skin

we purge ourselves of all light
when the day is over
we forget our names
when we sleep
– enter the mitosis
of dreams

we ignore the bones
thinning

never recognizing
how small colonies
of tissue
are lost
without a sound

Entwined

Your history
is tied around your waist
like a rope

you fling yourself
over the water
but the tire swing
beckons you back

you find a foothold
you don't find a foothold
it's always the same

the gravity
the incessant gravity
pulling you

you land wherever
the rope comes loose

you curse the murky water
for hiding
the tadpoles with broken tails
the moss that smothers your thoughts

nobody on the far edge
of the lake sees you

you go under
you become the body of water
you once hated

you are alone
you are not alone
you are the hue of
an unseen self

the water surrounds you
like the selective mutism
you had in second grade

the photosynthesis
keeps you holy
while you wait

Torrent

What if someone dropped you
in the middle of a river

what if you never knew
where the water came from –
if the snow pack was depleted

what if everyone told you
to go downstream
but everything inside you
told you "hold on"
to the boulder in the middle

what if you didn't
remember anything about water
not one word
that your science teacher
told you

what if you didn't the understand
the rapids
or how white water
spoke in its own dialect

the sediment from the bottom
gathers at your feet
you hear others
calling from the banks
but you lose consciousness

and when you wake
you find yourself
standing at the edge
of the estuary of night
the skyline
etched in ruined ink
and you

praying quietly
to a lone pelican
with the ocean's last fish
stuck in its throat

Estrangement

It's not like it happens
suddenly
you step off a curb
agree to take a little time away

maybe take a trip to another city

you look out the window of the bus
as the streets pass by

a few weeks go by
a small building collapses

then it's months
and a road buckles
and the signs reroute you
to a small town

a metal bridge sways
in the distance
you are not sure you can cross it again

you live in your house
made of clay and sin

every day
the river runs higher to the
underside of the bridge

and soon
twenty years of silence
has passed

you watch a burning city
from far away
and notice a pigeon flying towards you
gaining speed
pulling the sky's edges with it

finally landing
carrying its message
to an unmarked grave

Bent Sky

I watched the eclipse
from your gravesite

but I watched it
from the wrong angle

"remember the one
we saw in 1991"
I asked

I told you I missed you,
I told you the baby turned three,
and the house hasn't sold yet

but the grass
wasn't listening
and I couldn't think
of anything else to say

so I pulled out
my special glasses
"isn't it beautiful"
I said
and you nodded yes
from behind the sun

I only looked once
it's what you would have wanted

the rest of the day
I spent my time
meandering around the yard

pondering the
distortions of a bent sky
thinking about the moon
turning black

All My Wounds Are Self-Inflicted

The burn marks
on my brain
were born of
self loathing

my bones are calcified
from dilapidated memories

my finger nails
are cut down to the quick

I bind my legs
with a particular
length of rope

I practice
how to breathe through
self-persecution

It doesn't hurt anymore

anyone can wash their body
in a lather of scorn
that numbs the skin

I used to swear a blue streak
on purpose
because I knew my dad
would beat me first
and my smaller boned sister
would be protected
and instead
be sent to her room

I counted the bruises the next day
and was proud that I never cried

I could go to school
and tell everyone I fell off my bike
and tell everyone
how much it didn't hurt

Auto Immune

One part of the body
turns against the other

reacts as if an enemy
has invaded

the war against
friendly fire
goes on for years
possibly decades

one doctor
after another
gives pills in doses
unrecognizable to
your broken mouth

late at night you read
one medical article
after another

trying to understand
why the armed forces
attacked a sovereign
place in the body

you toss and turn
the siege goes on

you sleep
you love
you banish yourself
from your own bed

you watch yourself
line up words
inside your mind
a small army
encroaching
from afar

Fibromyalgia

The doctors say
the neurotransmitters
have lost their way

the grass has grown too tall
and covered a road
once known

they say
the language of synapse
is tinged with
a song too loud
a symphony gone mad

I tell them
I can tolerate high levels of pain
that I drank it as a serum
when I was young
why should it come back now?

I am up too late
reading about nerve paths
and the distorted intersection
of memory and myalgia

when even the stars
recede from the sky
I think about the napalm
released on these persecuted fields
and remember how
whole villages burned

Body Aches

When I sleep
for more than nine hours
my body aches all over
my bones
are preaching to me
about endings

During REM,
I see the cockroaches
that wait for me at the end of time
the sun that burns
through earth's crust
the insomnia that
suffocates the living

the wormholes
have made their way
through the coarse skin
of twilight
the small rivulets of day
run down my back

I try a heating pad
but the apnea of the galaxy
makes itself known

I try ice
but my muscles
convulse in the rhythm
of the Northern Lights

I tell myself
to stay in the present
but the threads of the cosmos
pull at me all morning

I pretend I am not
the sky breaking open
my mouth leaks
with the language of broken gods

my teeth incinerating themselves,
like stars
my tongue turning black

Fusion

They will take out the bad disc
clamp the space between

the bones will be one
your spinal cord finally
protected

there will be no way
to measure the fall out
the inventoried items
they will take from the body

they will make last minute
decisions when they "get in there"

There is no talk of how
you bent your neck to kiss me
on our first date
how it was all fluid then

each moment held apart
by measured spaces

three days after you are home
from the hospital
I think of those two vertebrae
once separate
now fused

slowly getting to know one another
the surfaces
absolving one another
as if there was anything
to forgive

Retinal Tear

The night before the operation
you go to the piano
in the dark
and play soft melodies
with your eyes closed

you tell me
you need to know
that if you lost your sight
you could still play

the notes drop
from the keyboard
to the floor
inside the cupboards
and beneath the bed

I pick up each one
hold them in my hands
and take them back to you
but I am too late

you are already asleep
I stand over you
make sure you are breathing steady
and the lamp is off

our room
fades to a shadow
of its former self

in the weeks that follow
I hear you after midnight
playing those same
incandescent chords
each one escaping
like a refugee
in the dark

Equinox

In Autumn
skin becomes
as heavy as a road

your footsteps in black shoes
are measured and prolonged

each turn of the pavement
takes you to a curb
a house you do not recognize
the address
a series of numbers
that do not follow
a logical sequence

finally, you see
the only prime number
streaked in white paint
and understand you
cannot be divided
by yourself

the last perennial tree
leans like an atheist
against the church window

you pull leaves
from your mouth
and watch them
pool by the storm drain

Between Twilight

Let's start with destruction
the decomposed bones
and walls collapsing after a strong wind

then go back
to how it was
before wholeness
before meteors
fell like rain

before shadows
understood their thirst
for light

before our bodies
became capsules
for sorrow

before you or I
had a name
and the nebulae and galaxies
accepted me
just as I was
broken
celestial

waiting for a small portal
in the world
waiting for a place to enter
a womb
that needed an opening
a place for the dust of stars
to reconfigure themselves
as me

Citadel

This is not your body
it does not belong to you
it is not the one
that left the sallow rooms of home
circa 1980
never to return

this is not the body
who entered the hallway
of a college dormitory
who carried English books
like a soldier carries ammunition

this is not the body
that left the same college town
pregnant with a son
with a man you knew
would someday leave

this is not the body
who gave birth and
bid farewell to a womb
who carried two babies

this is not the body
who falls into anesthesia
and counts the stitches like shame
this is not the body
you return to
each murky dusk

this is the body you were told to smite
this is the body you hid inside
this is the body you cradled

this is the body
that knows the sound of a belt
removed before a beating

this is the body that knows
how to leave
like a song rising from nothing
like music leaving a cathedral

Proceed with Caution

Assume
everything is contaminated

assume every surface
you touch
holds an invisible illness

you can spread it
without knowing

you are asymptomatic
but everyone
turns away

they can tell
that fear mutates
as quickly as a virus

the earth
whispered in your ear
long ago
"I will find you
I will find a way
to tell you when I've had
too much"

so you spend your days
looking for your own
antibodies
you search for them
in the soil
where you know
you will someday return

you sanitize your thoughts

you don't say anything to anyone
but you've had a sore throat
for fourteen days

the earth is having trouble breathing

there are no more ventilators

The House Is for Sale

I drove by today
and saw two strange men
working outside on the front yard
I wanted to run up to them
and tell
but I didn't

I drove home
and wondered how
a catalogue of crimes
breathing inside the rooms
can be buried

is there enough paint
to erase the scratch marks
on the walls

are there enough
small nails
to hold the secrets
beneath the floorboards

are there cracked rosaries
all over the house

are there old dresses
and dirty words
trapped inside the closets

are there pieces of me
dangling
from a few sparse hangers

Rape Whistle

After the support group
I fidget outside in the
November air

I fear
I have lost my keys again

a small framed woman
catches up to me
hands me the whistle,
forces it into my palm
and whispers
"in case"

I put it in my pocket
hold it in place, with one hand

I want to understand the shape
of mercy
how it can narrow itself
through a small silver chamber

I perseverate on how
the same instrument can be used
to coach football or track
or in this case
how to find other ways to run

I want to understand
how to remove a
grease tinged hand
from a sealed mouth

I want to know
how to sleep without
medication

I am given a list of "emergency contacts"

I want to ask the woman
"what does violation sound like
before it happens"

Rough Sex

Because
you never of thought of it
as rough

because even while inside you
he can't reach the part of you
that is holy

because if you asked him,
to let go of your wrists
he would

because begging for more
is always
consensual
even when your bones
are nailed to your own oppression

because
you said it was okay
while you were suffocating

because you still have
to sleep next to him

because there is a
gag order underneath the mattress

because your mouth
becomes an elegy
in the middle of the night

because there is a séance
embedded in the ritual
of sleep

and the night
will never tell you
how long it takes
to drown in your own starlight

Say It

Say you love it
say you love the way it hurts

say you wish he would just break you
and the concrete
will finally become dust

a stone
beats a stick to near death
and the splinters
are all that matter

lean back
say you need it
like an Adirondack chair
needs its slats separated

lean back at parties
while friends whisper in corners
about your strange affinity
and tolerance for pain

they don't understand
the frayed edges
of love and twine and rope and hate
or that masochism is born
within the rooms
you are carried to
against your will
"it hurts
it doesn't hurt
I don't take pain pills
I'm not suicidal very often"

repeat these self-made psalms
as if they were your body's retribution
for the years of self-exile

understand how
a falling stone
crushes a stick
merely because one
is heavier than the other

Sweet Tooth

I crave sweets after a big meal
especially after
I force myself to finish it all
because I know
the host is watching

It feels like pretending
you've enjoyed
a forced blow job

I move my silverware around
pray for dessert to come
I want something tangy but sweet
I hope it's lemon meringue pie

the host serves
chocolate souffle instead
I make myself eat it
I say it is delicious

I say I have a sore throat
and leave early

I buy oranges and tangerines
and lemons
at the fruit stand on the way home

In the kitchen
with the slanted floor
I remove the rinds
cut each open
like a fragmented truth

the next day
I bake pie after pie
after pie

I serve each piece
like a slivered lie

I tell everyone
I love to bake
It's important they know
how much I enjoy it

Pyromania

I carry pieces
of the fire with me
all day

I find ashes in my shoes
small fragments of flame
nestle themselves in my coat pocket

the morning rises like a black smoke
from which I cannot recover

I look for the culprit
in every crevasse of my clothing
but there is no answer

small planes still fly
over me
looking for sections of thick brush
and patches of smolder

sometimes I think about
the flat land
the way it was before we arrived
how seductive
how pristine

I return to moments of
dry lightning
how it lit up the sky
that one autumnal night
three decades ago

how the tree cracked open
and a slow methodical insanity
systematically
destroyed
everything in its path

Returning

When even the river
won't take you back

when you know
you are the orphan
of water

find solace
in the dry wood
the places where it's stacked
in the back shed

find the shadow self
in the cracked and open
fields of dry wheat

find the hayfield
where you sat for hours
when you were seventeen
just before you fled

find the unrepentant
asphalt roads
that led you to
the desert and its red clay
how it stuck
to the underside of your boots
for months
find the forensics
the quiet, still
music of dried blood

walk along the crumbling borders
of a river
carved by its own exile

As Glaciers Retreat, They Give up the Bodies and Artifacts They Swallowed

Smithsonian May 27, 2015

The lungs of the earth
are rising and falling

the places of hiding
soon to be extinct

a polar ice cap recedes
a black box is found
and the final words
of the crew and passengers
of the 1952 plane crash
spill out from the mouths
of strangers
from a near by island

the maps
in the all of the school rooms
are leaking salt water
the walls already ruined

your bed is floating
in a river of your own demise

there may be a day
you think of me
when another glacier
falls into the ocean

you will move to higher ground
and I will swim
into the rising sea

Snow Pack

When winter knows no prayer
and all the white birch
kneel before you

why won't you rise
when the widow of autumn
holds out her thin hand

why won't you
notice us
who are buried in the avalanche
of one another

emergency crews
rush to find us
we survive for days
on shrinking levels of oxygen

even when we are pulled from
dark tunnels
dawn breaks us in two

you leave us behind
in this cataclysmic wind

the rescue teams turn away

leaving behind

a terrain of regret

River Call

You took your boat
out on the Chehalis River
and caught sturgeon
with your brother
who was dying of pancreatic cancer

I think of you, father
holding up
the pre-historic looking fish
your hand in its mouth
and that half smile, half sneer

after twilight
you took us inside the cabin
put aside your Coors
cut the meat from bone,
and sawed through the coarse skin

you spoke to me
through gritted teeth
you told me
that soon the waters
would be too heavily fished
and there would be
too few sturgeon

you told me your own father used to
take you fishing before 5 a.m.
after a beating the night before

for years
after you climbed
out of our bunk beds
you left at dawn
with a car full of whiskey
and drove to the dark lake
near our home
searching for your ancient self
as if the fish
were still hiding from you
in that deep sandy bottom

Living the Days of Corona

The numbers change
by the hour
I check the web site
too often

I tell myself not to
watch the news
all the time

I wipe down my counter
instead

after dinner
I find a new graph
on the trajectory of deaths
in my region

I watch the curve spike
and see small images of people
falling off the back

like that scene in
Titanic
when everyone
fell off the ship

some to the ocean
some to the decks below
some plummeting
some holding on
some lonely
when the water
froze their stories in time

I try to sleep
all my meditation songs
fall below my bed

someone is being infected
someone is short of breath
someone remembers a prayer
they said when they were young

The Lie

When I was in second grade
I told a girl on the playground
that I lived in the hills
surrounding our town

I told her I lived with the wild animals
and I slept under a tree each night

for decades I never understood
why I told that lie
for decades
I forgot her name

now when I think about
my father
and his shadowy exits
and entrances into my room

I think I was trying to tell her
about claws
and teeth
and the sound of growling

that comes from behind a tree
I was trying to tell her
that I understood the sound
of brush rustling
in the distance
and how a small girl
figures out
how to hide
in abandoned caves,
learns how to stay still
so not a creature
can hear you breathe

these days
I scatter blessings
and dry leaves
amongst the mourning wolves

When I Was in Eighth Grade

I kept a list of everyone I hated at school
in my diary

occasionally
if someone was nice to me
I'd cross off their name

In winter, I discovered that my mother
went through my diary
she told me "I've never seen a child
with so much hate"
and she shook her head
and walked away

at home
I often beat up my older sisters
I hid in my bunkbed
I cut the eyes of my dolls

"she has such a bad temper"
they would say in other rooms

I didn't understand it either
my father loved me so much
he couldn't leave me alone

so much that
I was sequestered
in the slanted rooms where
all the doors disappeared

sometimes
when I kicked holes in the walls
my father would patch them up for me
I merely had to hand him the spackle
and he would smooth it all away

I can no longer find those old diaries
I have no lists
just a box in the garage
with some loose blank pages
and a doll I never named

It's Been Two Years

I have stopped
going to your grave site

it has not helped me
find a way to say goodbye

it is merely
another stone
etched in gray mourning

another testimony
to rotting flowers

another way
for my words
to boomerang

and it will be all my fault
again

I think I see the
soil turning itself under

I have walked in the
sharp spring grass
fallen to my knees
while no one else is watching

and when it's just
the two of us
again

I find
decades of conversations
stagnant water
around your tombstone

and still
nothing left to say

Two Deaths

When the person you ran *from*
and the person you ran *to*
die in the same month

you spend your time
examining the geology
inside a broken mountain

you spend time
setting up safe camps
in the dark night
calling for someone
to find you

you write "help"
across the legible places
of the sheered stone

you repel
against the flat wall
of yourself

you travel light,
drop the heaviest gear
down the steep cliff

and hope
you remember
how to find
the next foothold

High School Production of *Les Misérables*

Act I Scene 3   "Lovely Ladies"

I could tell the costume designer
was careful to dress the young girls
like old fashioned street hookers
who hid their money
where it belonged

no midriff
no fish nets
no shoes that broke their backs

each one pranced in
from stage left
each in a different shade of flawless red
sitting scantily upon the ancient props

but as the orchestra played
and their mouths opened
I could already tell the ones
who had been taken

those whose hips had been an altar

I could tell, those whose backs
had been pressed into the couch
with no stage crew looking on
only the fading lights
there was an ease to the
the way they arched their necks
dropped their gaze at the last minute
knew well the scripts of subservience

when the number was over
I folded my hands
hoping each girl would
scamper away quietly
and discreetly change her clothes

I waited for the scenes of war to come
for someone to die on stage
so the audience could finally grieve

Twenty Minutes into a Deep Sleep

You pull me off the couch
at midnight
to go outside
and witness the blood moon,
the lunar eclipse

I promised you I would get up
so I meander slowly outside,
half awake
until the crisp air enters my skin

we stare silent
your finger looped in mine

I wonder about prophecies
shaped like small swirls
of fog and shadow

we are watching the midnight sky
being broken and reassembled
all in a matter of moments

the tribunal of trees
hiding the edges of an unknown
forest of stars

the news stories say
"this is the *lunar* eclipse,
you can stare straight into it"

and we do
until gravity falls
back
onto itself

until I freefall beside you
as we sleep

the room dark
and iridescent
all at once

The Search

I am looking for the lamp
hoping it will
make itself apparent
in the nucleus of dawn

I am looking for hands
to reach the lamp

I am looking for the arms
that carry the hands
upwards
that will reach the light
like a torch
in an abandoned cave

I am looking for the body
that holds up the arms
who remembers how heavy
a book can be
right before you fall asleep

I am looking for
the chapter I lost
when the room closed its lids

I am looking for a morning
that will never arrive

I am praying
to a deity
I no longer believe in

I am dancing
around the room
with the conjugal visit
of regret

Dwelling

The money for the house sale
landed in your bank account today
I saw the dollar figure
and thought only
of a small yellow house
down a long gravel road
in Yuba county

I've saved all your paintings
and the portraits
you did not finish

I've saved all the letters
your parents wrote to you
in the 1950s

I don't visit your grave often enough
I trip over the divots
when the grass is wet
and land face forward
in places I am not welcome

I've saved the last seven dollars
from your wallet
it's the only part of your estate
that has not been inventoried
I called the water company
to cancel your account
and they told me the new family
is already there

I see them washing their hands
in your stainless steel sink

I see them opening the front door
when the sun comes up

I see them stacking firewood
for the long winter ahead

Somewhere in Yuba County

there is a woman
chopping wood
outside her yellow house
in the woods

she is eighty years old
and makes canned cherries
with her strong Danish hands

she knits after lunch time
and paints with oils
in the art studio she built
with her own hands

she remembers
her life as a child on the farm
and knows
she belongs in this wilderness

she calls to me
from hundreds of miles away

I wonder if she might be
taking a walk
down her long dirt road at dusk
stop to watch
the cougar she sees in the distance

she may wrap her pipes
as the cold snap comes

I put on one of her old sweaters
created from all the yarn
and the years
the hours
I will be without her

To My Twenty-Six-Year-Old Daughter

You are sitting in front of me
two days before my hysterectomy
telling me
you are having a baby in July
asking questions
only the moon can answer

the wooden grain in the kitchen table
runs in the same direction as the conversation

we sort through a thousand "ifs"
as the kitchen light flickers

I move a half empty glass
away from surgery instructions that tell me
"no food past nine, only a sip of water, no jewelry, no aspirin"

I am telling myself
I will be fine
all surgeons know
how to remove items from the body...

tumors
blockages
hidden prophecies

I am bidding farewell to a knotted house of cells
ramshackle after years of being empty
but it was your first home
your first warm universe
void of Saturn or satellites
where you held out your intricate hand
and stepped into your first dance with gravity

you
making your own constellations

you
forming, emerging
as celestial bodies do

quietly changing the galaxy
as if to say "I'm here"

After Days of Silence

When the wound opens
all that falls out
are swallowed words
thin as capillaries

your conversations are anemic
the transfusions
fade into a protracted night
of wounded sex

the transplanted
paragraphs
were not successful

the morphine drip
of meaningless apologies
seep into the sheets

you are alone
in a bed
holding the only known copy
of the do not resuscititate order
in your ghost-like hands

Ink

She took her pen
into the forest
and wrote long
sentences into the trees
until there were no more trees
and they succumbed
to the weight of description

soon after
she went to the river
and dropped paragraphs
into the water
and the rapids
carried her stories
downstream

she remained alone

with only the pen
and earth
now dry and barren
as the self
who carried her here

Guidelines in a Pandemic

Don't touch anything
not the doorknob
nor elevator button
or the jagged space
between
your cleaved lungs

wear a mask
to protect others
wear a mask
to hide your cyanotic self
the blue of your lips
the exact hue
of the ocean
we've smothered

don't let the
dead whale's carcass
float too close
to your bed

the small bits of plastic
inside the remains
will remind you
of dying
with plastic in your body

as if they
were trying to tell
their own story

and the body bags
washing up to shore
were not our own

Menu

I place a glass of wine
on the flat surface of forgiveness
and still nothing has moved

I place a bowl
of cut apples
on the windowsill
and refuse
to peel off the skins

I shred
the meat of a whole chicken
and leave the bones
on the countertop

I pull the
parsley and rosemary
and fresh roma tomatoes
from my small garden

and yet
I cannot find my mouth
I cannot find a way
to understand
why sustenance matters

when your teeth
are broken
because you mouthed off
one too many times

you will sequester your food
you will serve everyone
you will pretend you love dessert

you will imagine another table
another history
a way to fold and blend
your small, unrecognizable life
into a recipe you can
understand

Precision

Cut the crust edge
from your open mouth

fold the shape of the pie
into uneven edges
of remorse

wipe the flour from your
merciless lips

push the filling
into the dilapidated
sections of your throat

bake your body
at a temperature
only known for endings

and then forget
why you came into the kitchen
in the first place

Ritual

I put my day cream on
at night

I put my night cream on
in the day

I know it must be this way

I must find a way
to travel the two worlds
between the thin corridor
of dusk to dawn

I know it must be this way

so my skin
can recognize
itself
in either sphere
of the half light

Clean Up

When you pull
the saran wrap from the box
you watch the thin sheet stretch
beyond the width of your body
you hold the edge
keep it straight

you pull,
cut the seam
along the metal teeth
of a tattered box

you hold it in place
walk swiftly
to the plate of baked chicken
still slight with steam

but you don't make it that far
your finger slips
the plastic clings
in all the wrong places

reminding you of the evening's dinner
how you choked on unintended words

how you swallowed your own language
until it was a blend of sin and soliloquy

reminding you
of how a conversation
folds in on itself

how silence
is a mutation
of ordinary words

Waterway

It can be lonely
building a lake next to your house

You must say no
to social engagements

you must find a way
to eat your own loneliness
and make sure
no scraps are left behind

A simple bucket will not do
you must make small ponds
in the indents of your sadness
you must check water levels
every day

you will wait in a barren room
and nobody will know
you are hiding

as winter turns its back on you
you will finally walk close
to the body of water you've created

you will kneel at the sacrament
of its unknown depth

your sins will become
part of the runoff
from the rain

you will find contrition
in the braille of the wet soil

you will embrace the banished heretic
who has waited for you
in the clearing of absolved trees

The Wandering

The names on the street signs
fade
the words blend together
like children in a small hut

the lines in the road
fall beneath the asphalt

you walk around
looking for a familiar turn
in the road
a place you used to watch
the milk man drive by

you stare at strangers
and they look right through you

your skin is already translucent

you swore to yourself
you would not spend
too much time
looking for that same spot
on the sidewalk
where you stepped
on the crack
to break your mother's back

you didn't truly want to break it
or maybe not all the way

you just wanted her to remember
the endless years
of ping pong paddles
beating you to the floor
the spine that never healed

at night when you are speechless
you wonder
if a dying language
can be saved

"If There Were No Eyes in the World, the Sun Would Not Be Light" – Alan Watt

The map of the world
would not exist

our stories would be told
by the sounds of stones
by the tongues of a shaman

we would have to listen
for the footsteps of crows
and lean forward
to hear them building
their nests of oblivion

we would come to understand
rough water
by listening to the language
of a river folding in on itself

we would be unable
to build weapons for war
we wouldn't know
what an enemy looks like

we wouldn't know
how to tell time
or even understand
how a shadow
moves across a room

when all the earth's
borders were lost
we wouldn't know
we were gone

the blackness
would hold our hand
and we
would have to follow

Arc of Evening

A thousand moons
fracture the sky

the paleolithic timeline cracks
like a concrete bridge
after a catastrophic earthquake

the timeline
reverses itself
back to cro-magnon man
back to rock and stone and loneliness

back before Neanderthal man
before flint made fire
before Orion had a name

there were trees
who hid smaller creatures
there were swamps and fields
who find me when I am alone
swimming in the ancient creases of dark

I toss and turn –
take a pill to make me drift back

I use my opposable thumb to close
the prescription bottle

I enter the twisted sheets
as the medications take hold
I am immersed
in the secret rituals of sleep
from a tribe long ago
how a small child
will cry out when she is falling
and the sound will travel
across the worlds
across the rivers of mystery and shamanism

calling to me
like a century
that never saw itself burning

Love and Anthropology

Learn to love the skeletons
the ones standing in museums
far from home

the ones from science class
who stared at you
from across the room
while you dissected a frog
soaked in formaldehyde

love the intricate bones
the ones who prevail
and reside in closets

the ones
whose teeth are missing
with the bones chipped
in odd places

pay homage
to the ones found in tombs
holding the stories
of ancient kings and civilizations

rehearse a psalm
for the bones found
in a dry field of grass,
the only way to tell
a young girl's story
missing for years

speak to the spine,
it's eventual fracture

play love songs
in infinite dark rooms

hold up
your invariable hands
of dust
and satiate the earth
as any lover would

ACKNOWLEDGMENTS

I would like to acknowledge these journals (and their editors) for publishing the poems in this book, some in earlier forms:

One — "Floor Plan"
Atticus Review — "What to Say"
Split Rock Review — "Cooling Trend"
Third Wednesday — "The Fire is Ten Percent Contained"
Sweet Lit — "Bound to Repeat"
Boston Literary Magazine — "Entwined"
Cultural Weekly — "Torrent"
Lindenwood Review — "Bent Sky"
Two Bridges Review — "Body Aches"
Poeming Pigeons — "Fusion"
Slippery Elm — "Retinal Tear"
Califragile — "Proceed with Caution"
Cuthroat Magazine Truth to Power Anthology — "Rape Whistle"
Italian Americana — "Pyromania"
Chabot Review — "Returning"
About Place Journal — "As Glaciers Retreat They Give Up
   the Bodies and Artifacts They Swallowed"
Cultural Weekly — "Snow Pack"
Califragile — "Living in the Days of Corona"
Pirene's Fountain — "The Lie"
American Journal of Poetry — "When I Was in Eighth Grade"
Mocking Heart Review — "Two Deaths"

Oven Bird Poetry — "High School Production of *Les Misérables*"
Chiron Review — "Somewhere in Yuba County"
Mom Egg Review — "To My Twenty-Six-Year-Old Daughter"
Califragile — "Guidelines in a Pandemic"
Chiron Review — "Clean Up"
Cutthroat Magazine — "The Wandering"
Split Rock Review — "Arc of Evening"